# Confessions:
# The Truth About Perfect Timing

*a couples guide to reaching everything you desire in life*

OSCAR FRAZIER

KIYA D. FRAZIER

Cover and text designed by nDemand Consulting LLC, a strategy, marketing, and execution management consulting firm. (nDemandConsulting.com)

ISBN-10: 0615963463
ISBN-13: 978-0615963464

# References

Brown, Les. (Year Unknown). *Quotes by Les Brown.*
Evans, Tony. (2010). *The Covenant of Marriage.* Dallas: Dr. Tony Evans.
Henley, William Ernest. (1875). *Book of Verses.* London: D. Nutt.
Herbert, Frank. (1965). *Dune.*
Mays, Benjamin. (Year Unknown). *God's Minute.*

# PREFACE

Think back to when you were ten years old; think back to when you believed you could be anything you could think of, dream of or imagine. Whether you were a doctor, a policeman, or super-hero, do you remember how fearless you were? At ten years old you did what you loved, and believed that you could be anything you set your mind to.

So why don't we, as adults, have that same fearless spirit now? Today, too many of us allow doubts, fears, and excuses to control our life; we self-sabotage our dreams, passions, and goals. What would you do if you could get back those dreams, passions, and goals you gave up on 5 – 10 – 15 years ago? What would you do with the opportunity to reawaken the dreams that you've been putting on hold, because the timing just wasn't right? If you had the chance to ignite new dreams, would you take it?

In the pages following this preface you will find honest discussions, reflections, and tools that address the burning questions that you have deep inside. If you're dissatisfied with your life, your job, your career, this is the book for you. If you wake up each morning yearning for something more, this book is for you.

This book will give you advice on how to get past yourself, and make your dreams, passions, and goals a reality. Written from a married couples perspective, this book has a dual purpose to inspire the individual, as well as, inspire spouses/couples to support each other in their dreams and aspirations. There is no reference to gender in this book, as the dominant and supportive role in a relationship can shift between partners as various goals are pursued. It is our hope that you will find your inner fire in these pages; the fire you need to make your dreams come true.

OSCAR & KIYA FRAZIER

# CONTENTS

Dedication ...............................................................................iii

I. TIMING WILL NEVER BE RIGHT .............................................1
   Spouse 1 Reflection ..........................................................1
   Spouse 2 Reflection .......................................................11

II. PASSION SUICIDE (BECOMING COMPLACENT) ...............18
   Quick Story.......................................................................18
   Observation ....................................................................19
   Couples Support .............................................................22
   Bring it Full Circle ........................................................24

III. FEAR (THE DREAM KILLER) ...........................................29
   Forced to Conform .........................................................29
   Afraid to Ask for What You're Worth ..........................31
   Overcoming Fear.............................................................32
   Empower Each Other Through the Fears....................34

IV. WHAT ARE YOU WAITING FOR? .....................................36
   Quick Story.......................................................................36
   Couples Support .............................................................37
   Money or Time ................................................................41

V. THE WEALTHIEST PLACE ON EARTH ..............................44
   Die On "E"..........................................................................44
   Introspective Analysis ..................................................46

VI. YOU'VE DECIDED TO TAKE THE LEAP, SO NOW WHAT? ........53
   The Leap of Faith............................................................53
   The Challenge to Let Go................................................56

VII. 86,400 SECONDS .............................................................58
   Be Accounted For ...........................................................58
   Productivity Schedule ...................................................62

VIII. BEING RELENTLESS ......................................................64
   Average Won't Get It ......................................................64
   At Your Core.....................................................................66

ABOUT THE AUTHORS ...........................................................71

OSCAR & KIYA FRAZIER

# Dedication

We'd like to dedicate this book to our parents. They have shown us a great example of what hard work and dedication should look like.

We also want to dedicate this book to "you" (the reader) as it is our hope this book inspires you to follow your dreams and passions.

With Love & Humility,

Oscar & Kiya Frazier

OSCAR & KIYA FRAZIER

# I. TIMING WILL NEVER BE RIGHT
## Spouse 1 Reflection

We were at the top of our careers. In 2011 and 2012 combined, I managed to earn just shy of $600,000 (gross) and life just couldn't seem to get any better. We were happy, could do just about what we wanted and the sky was [seemingly] the limit.

We got married January 21st, 2012 via destination wedding in Maui, Hawaii and only invited our "close" friends and family. Albeit, several of our friends were not in the financial position to make a trip like this, and we only planned on paying for our immediate family, so our wedding was very intimate. We spent two weeks in Maui and spent many of the nights during our honeymoon planning what the next 1-3-5 year plan would look like (Yes, I was one of "those" type of people that tried to plan everything). Our plan discussion(s) shifted from when we'd have kids, to who should leave corporate space first (we'll get to that later), to how many bedrooms the house we'd purchase would have, to that convertible and boat I wanted (which I am so glad I didn't purchase ☺). During the day, we'd spend time touring the towns and taking long excursions through the beautiful streets. Before we knew it, two weeks were just about up and it was time to get back to reality.

As much as I've flown, I have never been a fan of the feeling I get when I fly (you know, the light-headed feeling or stomach drops whenever the air changes or we hit turbulence), so I tried my best to talk to my partner as much as possible. Keep in mind, a flight from Maui back to Charlotte, North Carolina is approximately 9 hours so there's plenty of time to talk (or sleep like my partner can amazingly do on airplanes). During the flight, I went through hundreds upon hundreds of emails and did my best to ignore the fact that we were leaving paradise and headed back to the fast-paced, hustle and bustle of the management consulting industry. At the time, I was responsible for the largest Statement of Work that the company had ever won. Its value was approximately $23 million. Prior to our trip to Maui and our getting married there were rumors circulating that my client may be ramping down which meant ending the contract early. However, I thought that I could find a way to add enough value to the project that would influence my client to keep the Statement of Work rolling.

We arrived back in Charlotte on the morning of Monday, January 30th, 2012. We left the airport and headed straight to the dog kennel to pick up our boxer Apollo who had been boarded during our wedding and honeymoon. When we got to the house, we [slowly] unpacked and began to get back in to real-world mode. It hit us both that we were not the same couple that had left the house two weeks earlier; we were married – a unit – a team. My partner began going through hundreds of emails and responding as appropriate. I sat with Apollo and went through my bank account transactions online to see just how much we spent during our honeymoon (wasn't too bad). Day went to night, and we were now one day away from having to return to work.

Tuesday, January 31st, 2012 was a bit of a blur. I remember calling a few direct reports to get a few high-level updates about my programs and projects that were currently underway. I was back in work mode, and ready to regain control of my portfolio. Morning quickly turned to night and it was time to return to work.

Wednesday, February 1st, 2012 was our first day back to work from honeymoon and we both decided to work from home. I was working in the living room, and my partner was working in the makeshift office. My partner came out of the home office and notified me about being pulled in to a "random" 15-minute meeting with Human Resources and the line of business executive for later that day. I thought it a little strange, but didn't think much of it. Several meetings, calls, and follow-ups occurred throughout the day, and before we knew, it was time for the "random" 15-minute meeting.

My partner always shuts the door in whatever room a call is taking place because I have a tendency to eavesdrop and mouth my opinion of the conversation and it interferes with staying focused. I was limited in what I could hear during the 15-minute meeting, but what I saw next told me everything I needed to know. My partner opened the door of the makeshift home office and the energy from that room hit me like a ton of bricks. Our eyes locked and I saw the words before it could come out my partner's mouth. "They fired me," my partner said. My heart dropped. Ya-see, our 1-3-5 year plan outlined during our trip to Maui suggested that I would be the first one to step away from corporate space to pursue our entrepreneurial endeavors. How could they just "fire" my partner? For heaven's sake, we just got married!

I sat there, looked my partner in the eyes and said, "well it's time to start building out and launch that non-profit we've been talking about". At the time, I didn't know whether to be angry, upset, scared, or poker-faced. The thing that came naturally at that time was to be forward-moving and poker-faced.

A couple of months went by and it began to sink in that my partner's life had substantially changed. I was now still working at the same company, in the same executive role, but also trying to launch a non-profit that I wasn't sure would work. The next several months (i.e., February through about May 2012) were very bumpy for us. Several arguments and misunderstandings took place, primarily around getting our non-profit off the ground successfully. The other factor was us deciding to put our plan to buy our first house together on hold, and deciding to buy a one-bedroom condo in uptown Charlotte until we had better footing and could get back on the 1-3-5 year plan that was rocked on February 1st.

Fast-forwarding a few months, we managed to successfully launch the non-profit, purchased our one-bedroom condo in cash, and made it through all of the arguments and misunderstandings…all in our first 5 months of marriage. But, what about my plan to leave corporate space? Is this still an option? Can a newlywed couple sustain without a steady paycheck? Some of the questions that crossed my mind as June 2012 approached.

The second half of 2012 was very difficult for me. Remember earlier in this chapter I mentioned my inclination that the twenty-three million dollar Statement of Work may be ramping down earlier than anticipated? Well it was happening. I was responsible for letting go approximately 146 contractors spanning across the United States, and it had to be done immediately. The next months of 2012 (approximately June-July) were traumatic and full of emotional rollercoasters; both at work and at home (Note: I hadn't quite figured out yet how to leave work at work).

Since 2004, I provided high-level strategy consulting services to small businesses or aspiring entrepreneurs, but never incorporated it as a business. Friends and family would come to me for help with business plans or strategic planning for their endeavors, and [most of the time] I'd provide free services/advice. When the end of July 2012 approached, I found myself at the lowest point of my career. I had just let go of approximately 146 people who had families and [in many cases] were the only source of income in their households. I could relate now. I had grown bitter with the "big company" mentality and was ready to begin planning my exit strategy. In early August 2012, I decided to incorporate the services I provided to friends and family, naming it nDemand Consulting LLC, a strategy, marketing, and execution firm.

As you know by now, I'm a plan-the-plan kind of person, so I created this one year corporate space exit strategy, in which I would wait to leave my existing job until I had enough clients (or at least pipeline) to sustain with nDemand Consulting as our primary source of income. After losing that twenty-three million dollar Statement of Work with our client, the same client began changing its model and significantly cut more Statement of Works. This ultimately led to my portfolio of programs and projects moving from approximately $46 million, to less than $3 million (and falling). My line of business executive told me I had nothing to worry about and we'd get back to where we were in no time. Be that as it may, I saw a very different picture.

Anxiety was high at home. All I talked about was how inevitable it was that I would be let go soon because there wouldn't be enough profit to pay for everyone's salaries. As time went on, nDemand Consulting and our non-profit was growing [very] slowly, and all we could do was save as much money as possible with the anticipation that I would also be unemployed soon. It was October 15th, 2012. I got an invite on my calendar for a "random" 15-minute meeting.

I was in the office on Monday, October 15th, 2012 and saw the Human Resources executive (normally in mid-west office) in our office working in a conference room. I stopped by the conference room she was in and said, "Good morning, what brings you to Charlotte today". She mentioned that she had a couple important meetings, but nothing specific. I didn't think much of it and continued down the hall to my office. Five minutes after sitting down, I got the invite for the 15-minute "random" meeting. I accepted the meeting invite, which was scheduled to occur shortly. I answered a few other emails and prepared myself for a normal meeting with Human Resources and my line of business executive. I walked in the same conference room I stopped by moments ago to say good morning to my Human Resources executive, and could immediately feel the energy in the room. I sat down with my pen and pad ready for instruction. "We regret to inform you that, effective immediately, we have to let you go as we are no longer in a financial capacity to sustain your role". I sat there in total disbelief, but went with the "forward-moving", "poker-face" look I had given my partner when the same conversation was had in February 2012. I signed my letters, accepted my severance package, and packed my belongings.

As I sat in my office reality seized the moment. I asked myself one simple question: "are you ready to take on the world without a safety net?" I then stood up and looked out my [soon-to-be-old] office window at the beautiful Charlotte skyline and said to myself, "I'm ready". Tears ran down my face and all that would come to my mind was a poem I learned back in 2002 entitled Invictus, by William Ernest Henley. I began to recite it: *"Out of the night that covers me, black as the pit from pole to pole, I thank whatever Gods may be, for my unconquerable soul. In the fell clutch of circumstance I have not winced nor cried aloud. Under the bludgeoning of chance, my head is bloody, but unbowed. Beyond this place of wrath and tears looms but the horror of the shade, and yet the menace of the years finds and shall find me unafraid. It matters not how strait the gate, how charged with punishments the scroll, I am the master of my fate; I am the captain of my soul."* I soberly wiped the tears from my eyes, cleared my throat, called my partner, and said "are you ready to pursue our passions full time?" There was a pause, and then an answer, "come on home".

The remainder of 2012 and 2013 was the most empowering. We sat in the house together planning and putting ideas in to action. Life becomes different when there's no safety net. We knew that the sky was truly the limit now and all we had to do was apply ourselves. All of the experience and preparation in corporate space was leading to this moment – this time – this destination. The matter in which we got there was irrelevant to the fact that we arrived. By the beginning of 2013, we were landing small business clients and making an impact one small business at a time. In hindsight, I often wonder if we'd still be "planning the plan" in 2014 (when this book was written) versus pursuing our passions. Waiting for the perfect time is a sure way to comfort excuses. Sometimes it takes getting knocked down to bring the best out of you.

## Spouse 2 Reflection

January 30th, 2012, I was on an amazing high. We just got back from a wonderful honeymoon in Maui. I was feeling refreshed and ready to take on the world. Life was pretty good. I was excited to begin this new stage of life with my partner. My career was heading in the right direction. Did I love my place of employment? No. However, I was well-paid. My job allowed me the freedom to work remotely, and there was no micro-manager over my shoulder everyday. I reported directly to the VP of Marketing. I knew someday I would own my own company, but for now I was content climbing the corporate ladder. It was safe. I was comfortable. Why rock the boat? Sure my partner and I had talked about entrepreneurship. We had great pillow talks about building our empire. We even planned our escape. I would remain in corporate for a few more years, while my partner would begin to pursue our first business venture. Once business number one was up and running, I would say my goodbyes to a 9-to-5, and then step into my entrepreneur suit. We thought we could plan everything out, but little did we know our safely planned existence was about to be dealt a serious blow.

February 1st, 2012, we'd only been back from the honeymoon for two days. We hadn't quite recovered from jet lag. We decided to work from home as we tried to get back in the swing of things. It was mid-morning when I got a meeting invite from my VP of Marketing for a quick 15-minute touch-point call. I thought it a little odd at first, but didn't waste too much time on it as I accepted the invite. It was an hour or two later when my phone rung. It was an office number, but one I didn't recognize. I answer, "Hello". On the other side was a Human Resources Representative, and my VP of Marketing. My heart sunk and an uneasy feeling came over my head and perched itself on my shoulders. I tried to shake off the feeling and tried to rationalize what this call was about in my head. I was working on re-branding several of our social media policies. Maybe this call was about that. However, deep down I knew exactly what the call was about. I was being let go.

Though that exact moment was clear, I didn't see it coming. I went through a rollercoaster of emotions during the call; anger, fear, frustration, and disappointment. My head was running a marathon. I felt like I had stepped outside my body as I watched everything unfold. Though I was on fire, I kept a professional tone while these two individuals turned my world upside down. They didn't care that I had just gotten married. They didn't care about my well-being or the well-being of my partner. Their demeanor during the call was cold; strictly business. So, why fuss with them, why waste my energy pleading my case? Their minds were already set, and by the time the phone disconnected they would be on to the next thing. "Ok, well thank you for the opportunity...no, I have no questions at this time," were the only words I could dig up to say as my comfortable 9-to-5 security blanket was ripped from my hands.

Telling my partner that I had lost my job was a bit more challenging. I couldn't get the words out my mouth fully before tearing up. What about our plans? What about the discussions we had? My partner was supposed to be the one to leave corporate first. We had set goals; we were on track to purchase a wonderful house, start a family, save, and *then* start our businesses. Here we were newly-weds, fresh off of our honeymoon, and now we'd have to deal with a major household change not even two weeks into our marriage. It was hard. I was angry. I wanted to kick something, punch something, yell and scream, but there was no time for that. I spent the rest of the evening discussing next steps with my partner. Though I knew both our heads were spinning with emotion, my partner didn't seem to miss a beat. There was no time to be upset and vent about what just happened. The very next day I buckled down in front of my computer and began the process of revamping our non-profit organization for an official launch in May 2012.

My life had changed drastically. I hid all the confusion flowing through my mind and channeled all my energy into building our non-profit.

March and April would become a fast pace whirlwind of meetings, brainstorming sessions, arguments, and stress. My partner was juggling his executive responsibilities at work, with co-founder responsibilities for our non-profit. Things at work weren't great, which made matters worse. My partner's portfolio was falling apart due to one client's company-wide reorganization. Our conversations became solely focused on what was happening at work, or what was happening with the non-profit. There was little time for us to enjoy each other. My partner began to worry and stress everyday about job security. Then as projects ramped down, my partner was responsible for telling over one hundred people that they were loosing their jobs, with no support from the company's Human Resources department. All of the turmoil from the workplace spilled over into our personal lives in which we normally enjoyed security, happiness, and laughter. Instead we were forced into survival mode and the need to succeed.

In the next few months we scaled back our plans to purchase a house. We did a cash purchase for a nice one-bedroom condo in uptown Charlotte, NC. Our rationale was the new property was in the city (where we did all our work, meetings, etc.), and it was ours. We owned it; we'd have a solid roof over our head no matter what.

May 2012, Sound Decisions RDS, Inc. a 501c3 non-profit organization is officially launched in Charlotte, NC. The event is a success, with several community leaders, business owners, influential Charlotteans, and friends and family in the audience. The road here was paved with many arguments and stress on the home front, but on that night we smiled and enjoyed reaching a milestone successfully.

Fast-forward, the date is October 15th, 2012. After many months of worry, lay-offs, and stress my partner received an invite for a quick 15-minute touch-point meeting with his executive and Human Resources. I remember getting the call. "Hey, it's me, come pick me up, they just let me go," my partner explained. The voice on the other end of the phone was calm and relaxed. It almost sounded like my partner was smiling through the phone. To be honest it was one of the happiest sounds I had heard in 8 months. I responded, "I'm on my way," I grabbed the keys and headed out the door.

I'm telling you all this to simply show you that no matter how much you plan for the perfect time to follow your dreams, your passion, your future – life happens. The timing will never be perfect. Stop waiting for the perfect time and make it now. Don't wait for a chain of events to knock you on your rump, before finding your purpose for being. I truly believe that if I hadn't been let go from my job I would have remained content. I would have never taken the steps to become an entrepreneur, or even write this book. I would have kept going to a 9-to-5 and been okay with helping someone else build their dream company. In reality, I wasn't built to be content; I am designed to be great! Each of us is designed to be great. The crazy thing is we set limits on ourselves mentally, physically, and emotionally.

The remainder of this book seeks to encourage, empower, and inspire you to take that leap of faith. Whether it is entrepreneurship, pursuing your passion, relationship based issues, career advancement, or setting goals; you can and will do it!

## II. PASSION SUICIDE (BECOMING COMPLACENT)
### Quick Story

So remember how I said we were landing small business clients in the beginning of 2013? I forgot to mention the part about the peaks and valleys. When you and your partner are pursuing a passion/goal, it will be easy (and almost natural) to want to go back to what you're used to. When we were no longer in the corporate space working for someone, we would get calls and emails constantly from other large firms looking to recruit us, which would have returned us back to the tax bracket we were in during 2011 and 2012. Let me be the first to say, a couple of missed checks certainly doesn't make it easy to turn down a quarter-million dollar salary. I truly believe difficult times encountered in the beginning during the pursuit of your passion/goals are a true testament to how determined you are to succeed. In hindsight, there would have been some things I would have done differently as the passion/goal-owner relevant to how I communicate with my partner.

## Observation

There are many people in this world that cannot stomach the idea of working in an office for the rest of their lives. The idea of being forced to work for a set number of hours, with set times for lunch and breaks, in a specific place is incredibly stifling. What's fueling this growing mentality? I believe it stems from the fact that most people today are extremely unsatisfied with their jobs. Now I know there are pockets of people out there who truly love what they do, and maybe even enjoy the nine to five lifestyle, but these people are progressively becoming the minority.

Why is that? Why are people becoming more dissatisfied with what they are doing at work? After some deep conversations with friends, family, and countless professionals, I've come to what I believe is the core of this dissatisfaction. People simply are becoming more dissatisfied with work because it doesn't allow them to enjoy the rest of their lives. The constant forty (or more) hours per week spent doing something that they're not passionate about leaves them burnt out, with barely enough energy left for anything else like family or friends. Tell me if this is your typical workday:

- Wake up earlier than you'd like (struggle to get going).
- Rush to get out the door, only to get caught in traffic (let the stress begin).
- Sit at your desk all day solving problems and issues that you really don't care anything about (more stress).
- Go home, throw some kind of meal together fast (usually something pre-cooked, or frozen) because you're exhausted.
- Turn on the TV because you're too tired to think about anything else.
- Go to bed (usually later than planned).
- Start the cycle all over again (Repeat).

Does this sound about right? Of course if you're married and/or have children there are a few more steps involved, which can be even more exhausting. I refuse to believe that this is the life that we were designed to live. Life was built to be enjoyed and savored; but the truth is many of us are just here going through the motions. I like to call it "working for the weekend".

So why aren't more people pursuing their passion? Why aren't more people centering their lives on something they enjoy doing? Here are some of the most common excuses:

1. What am I passionate about?
2. I don't have anyone to go to for advice, encouragement, or support.
3. I don't know how to make money from my passion.
4. Work is just a part of life.
5. What if I fail?
6. I have a family and a mortgage that I'm responsible for.
7. Between my current job, my family, kids activities, and other things I have to do, where am I going to find time to pursue my passion?
8. It's too risky. In this economy, I need job security.

This list could go on and on. The truth is everything listed here is an excuse; and excuses lead to passion suicide (hence the name of this chapter). Someone once told me that excuses are the most dangerous thoughts in the world. Do you see your excuse in this list? You should circle it, write it down, and then do some research on it. I bet you'll find two or more ways to get around it. It makes no sense to place a false hurdle in front of your passions and dreams. Find someone that's already doing it and learn how he or she did it. Figure out your strengths; ask friends, family, a mentor, or business associates what they believe are your gifts. My point is don't settle for the excuse; you and I both know you can do better.

## Couples Support

*"Marriage is a covenantal union designed to strengthen the capability of each partner to carry out the plan of God in their lives."* - Dr. Tony Evans

Sharing your dreams and passions with your partner is very important. You both, at some point, should play the role of the dream pursuer and the supporter. Your marriage should empower you to realize and accomplish your purpose here on earth. As the supporter your job is not simply to verbally express your support, but to physically and mentally support your partner's passion(s). It's unfortunate that marriage can, and often times, will have the opposite effect if partners are not supportive. Make sure you're taking advantage of the power that you have to uplift and empower him/her. Avoid these common mistakes:

1.  Doing nothing. It's not your passion - as a partner and dream supporter you shouldn't have any problem helping your partner research ways to pursue and/or improve their passion (e.g., even helping them set up for events or tradeshows). Simply asking, "what can I do to help?" goes a long way.

2.  Using discouraging words - as a partner and dream supporter our words are powerful. One or two words can be the difference between your partner feeling empowered or disheartened.

3.  Not compromising or being willing to make sacrifices - So your partner is not quite ready to walk away from the nine to five. We know household finances are a huge part of this decision. The best way to help is simply by being willing to pick up the slack at home in the evenings and/or weekend.

This will give your partner more time to devote toward their goals, and could potentially mean the difference between them being able to pursue their passion fulltime in the near future.

For those of us who are married, we depend on our partners more than anyone else. If we're not mutually supportive of our dreams and passions, neither partner will make progress toward their intended goals. Every moment you free your partner up to pursue their dreams, you are serving them; and I'm sure they will be quick to return the favor.

## **Bring it Full Circle**

What motivates you? What keeps you going when everything in you says to quit? If you could do anything you want and not have money be a concern, what would it be? Merriam-Webster defines *passion* as "a term applied to a strong feeling of enthusiasm or excitement for something or about doing something". Have you ever noticed when you ask someone about their profession or "job" it is usually vastly different from their passion? Why is this so?

To some, a passion is synonymous with a figment of

imagination. Have you said or heard someone else say: "what pays the bills is job X, but if I had it my way, I'd love to do Y" or "I'd love to do Y if I can only find a way to make money doing it"? If so, you're not alone. Most people are, by default, driven by taking care of their basic necessities first, before doing anything outside of the box. In Maslow's Hierarchy of Needs, it is described that the two baseline levels of motivation in people are physiological needs (e.g., air, food, water) and safety needs (e.g., body / personal security, financial / employment security, etc.). At a young age, most people are taught that a "job" will pay you money, which will help you keep and sustain your baseline needs. An alternative way of thinking may be to teach (at a young age) people to find what makes them happy and help them strive to grow deeper in those areas. Let's take a look at the effects of not pursuing your passion(s) from a relationship perspective.

Before you decide to pursue your passion, ensure your partner is "in the know". As the passion or goal-owner, it is critical that you clearly communicate to your partner why this passion/goal is important to you, and how you want him/her to be a part of your transformation in pursuing it. Here's an easy exercise to get you ready to articulate your passion/goal to your partner:

1. **Prepare**: on a sheet of paper, write out your passion/goal succinctly.

   a. Example I: I have a passion/goal to *become an entrepreneur in the area of management consulting.*

   b. Example II: I have a passion/goal to *lose weight.*

2. **Quantify**: on the same sheet of paper, write out a timeline of when you will meet your passion/goal.

   a. Example I: I will accomplish this passion/goal by *having one client by the third quarter of 2014.*

   b. Example II: I will accomplish this passion/goal by *losing 25 pounds by the end of 2014.*

3. **Qualify**: on the same sheet of paper, write out how you are qualified or how you will get qualified to pursue this passion/goal.

   a. Example I: I will meet this passion/goal by *using my existing management consulting experience to form my own firm.*

   b. Example II: I will meet this passion/goal by *setting up a few free consultations with fitness coaches and signing up with the one that presents the best options for me.*

4. **Include**: on the same sheet of paper, write out how and why you want your partner to help you pursue your passion/goal.

   *a.* Example I: As you are an important part of my life, I need you to help me reach my passion/goal *by helping me develop a business plan and marketing materials.*

   b. Example II: As you are an important part of my life, I need you to help me reach my passion/goal by *helping me research local fitness coaches.*

5. **Bring it Full Circle**: put the "Prepare, Quantify, Qualify, Include" steps in to a succinct communication.

   *a.* Example I: *I have a passion/goal to become an entrepreneur in the area of management consulting. I want to measure my progress by having one client by the third quarter of 2014. I will meet this passion/goal by using my existing management consulting experience to form my own firm. As you are an important part of my life, I need you to help me reach my passion/goal by helping me develop a business plan and marketing materials. Will you help me?*

b. Example II: *I have a passion/goal to lose weight. I want to measure my progress by losing 25 pounds by the end of 2014. I will meet this passion/goal by setting up a few free consultations with fitness coaches and signing up with the one that presents the best options for me. As you are an important part of my life, I need you to help me reach my passion/goal by helping me research local fitness coaches. Will you help me?*

Now that you've articulated your passion/goal, it's time to put some action to your words. Take the same "Bring it Full Circle" statement you wrote out in the exercise above and bring it down to smaller chunks that you and your partner can handle. The best aspect of you reaching your passion/goal is that you will not be alone. Your partner is there to support you and help you achieve your passion/goal. Whenever you feel complacent or "too busy" to keep pushing toward your goal, go back to your "Bring it Full Circle" statement and repeat it until you feel motivated to continue.

## III. FEAR (THE DREAM KILLER)

*"I must not fear. Fear is the mind-killer. Fear is the little-death that brings total obliteration. I will face my fear. I will permit it to pass over me and through me. And when it has gone past I will turn the inner eye to see its path. Where the fear has gone there will be nothing. Only I will remain."* - Frank Herbert

*"Fear is a tiny little evil that disintegrates you from within. You must learn to face it; you must learn to control it…if you're scared, say you're scared!"* - Unknown (modified)

### Forced to Conform

When I was in corporate America I did what worked. I played in the sand box nicely with all the other kids, just like I was taught.

I worked hard, didn't make waves, and conformed to company culture. It worked, I was very successful, well paid, and was climbing that wonderful corporate ladder. There were times when I wanted to inject my creativity, or sound the alarm that there were other unique ways to do the things we were doing, but I knew better. Company culture didn't like a loose canon. So I stayed in the pocket and performed. It was comfortable and secure, so I thought.

So why did I feel like my creativity was being stomped out? Why did I feel like I was running on a treadmill? Deep down inside I wanted more than just security. I wanted to live; not simply survive. It wasn't until later that I would realize the difference. Fear of the unknown will force a person to do what works. Fear will cause a person to operate in survival mode for their entire life.

Fear is the root of procrastination and the breeding grounds for self-doubt. Have you ever heard the saying, "doubt kills more dreams than failure ever will"? The truth is we don't fail because we don't pursue; we let fear and doubt rule. If you have a passion, a goal and a dream right now, what's stopping you? Let me guess;

doubt, right? Doubt will stop you from taking a trip, going on a date, taking a course to further your education, trying a new hairstyle, hiring a personal trainer, supporting your partner's dreams... going for it, whatever *it* may be.

## Afraid to Ask for What You're Worth

I remember the first time a potential client asked me how much it costs to complete a business plan for their organization. I immediately froze. I spent over a decade of my career putting together proposals and pricing sheets for corporate giants and easily billing my consulting services out to clients at $250+ per hour, but found myself afraid to state the value I felt I brought to the table for this small startup client. I remember saying to the potential client, "let me take back your request to the team and I'll get the price back to you" (note: what team? It was just my partner and me at the time...anyway, back to the point).

I got home and told my partner, "I think we just landed our first real client, but I have no idea what to charge". My partner laughed and asked how I could not be sure when that's all I did for over a decade (i.e., pricing and proposals). I replied, "Yes, but you don't understand…this is different. They aren't used to paying that much for a person like me" (note: as if I were the only small business consultant in the world ☺). I spent the remainder of the day researching price points for business plans, and kept finding prices I felt were substantially higher than the value of a business plan. I finally got the courage to craft my first Statement of Work with the nDemand Consulting brand on it and submitted it to the client. Within an hour, the Statement of Work was signed and we were in business.

## **Overcoming Fear**

The best way to overcome fear is to prepare for success. Do you remember the feeling you had walking in to a classroom to take a test that you've fully studied for, versus walking in to a classroom to take a test that you have not studied for? When you've properly prepared for the test, there's a feeling of confidence that is so strong, there's little (if any) room for fear or second-guessing. The same applies to overcoming fear in starting and/or accomplishing your passion/goal. For example, if you're starting a business or pursuing entrepreneurship, take the time to conduct the proper research and ask the 3 "Will-Is My-Do" series of questions:

1.  Will there be enough people to buy the product/service I'm offering?

2.  Is my product/service competitively priced enough so people will buy it?

3.  Do I have a way to bring the people who may be interested and my product/service together consistently?

The "Will-Is My-Do" series of questions will serve as a basis for the researching process. Once you have solid answers for these questions, you will notice a shift in your fear level.

The next best way to overcome fear is to stop being afraid of failure. Though we don't plan for failure, we must understand how to recover from it and move forward. Almost every successful mogul experienced failure during his/her journey to the top, and would've guaranteed continued failure if they gave up. Embrace failure as an opportunity to learn more, become wiser, and develop "war stories". When you and your partner look back over a successfully reached passion/goal and can smile/chuckle at some of the mistakes made, it will all be worth it.

## **Empower Each Other Through the Fears**

If you're married ask yourself are you weighing your partner's dreams down with your fears and doubts. Sometimes we allow our fears and doubts to seep into how we communicate and support our partner. So your partner comes to you and expresses that it has been one of their life-long dreams to open a small mom-and-pop restaurant. Do you instantly begin thinking about all the things that could go wrong, start worrying about where the money is going to come from, or think we can't do that right now as we've got so many other responsibilities. Well this is the perfect explanation of how you can kill your partner's dreams with your fear and doubts.

Far to often, we let fear and doubt kill our dreams. Not anymore. Whenever you feel afraid of doing something, or even your partner doing something, question where the fear is coming from. Is it real, or imagined? If you're not in any perceived physical danger, what are you afraid of? Are you afraid of making a mistake? Then strive for excellence not perfection. Are you afraid of losing status? Think of how much more you stand to gain as you stretch your potential. Are you afraid of the unknown? Stop planning your life away. I'll testify that the unexpected twists have brought my partner and I the most joy, and actually taken us down a path that's better than what we could've dreamed. I believe James Allen said it best in As a Man Thinketh, "A person is limited only by the thoughts that he chooses." Beyond the natural fear we are born with (i.e., the fear of falling and the fear of loud noises) every other fear has been learned. You have to push through your uncertainties. Your dreams depend on it.

## IV. WHAT ARE YOU WAITING FOR?
### <u>Quick Story</u>

I vividly remember a candid conversation with a boss I had in 2004 when I was living in Norfolk, Virginia and working for a financial services institution. I had spent (approximately) two weeks creating spreadsheets and reports for a team meeting in Concord, California my boss and I were traveling to. I noticed every time I swung by my boss' office, he was always laughing and talking on the phone with his kids and wife. I grew frustrated and felt over-worked and under-valued. After making the fifth revision to a spreadsheet that contained approximately three thousands lines of data, I'd had enough. I looked my boss straight in the eyes and asked him, "so what do you do around here? I work sometimes until midnight in the office and I watch you go home everyday right at 5pm." My boss chuckled and leaned back in his chair. He replied, "As long as I have employees like you that are willing to keep me looking good in front of my direct reports and executives, there's no need for me to work hard." At that very moment, I understood the difference between fulfilling my dreams, and fulfilling someone else's.

## **Couples Support**

On several occasions, my partner and I talked about what it would be like to have our own company. How great it would be to control our destiny and shape our lives, our money, our free time, etc. We went on about the "what if's" and the "when we's". Then day after day we put it off, returned to our comfortable corporate existence, and buried ourselves in our work. Our number one reason for not doing something right then always seemed to be time-driven.

What is the number one reason that you are not following your dream today? What exactly is it that you are waiting for? Write it down. Have your partner write down their reason as well. Now share it. That's right share it with your partner, a friend, the universe; say it out loud. Now fold up that piece of paper, get a lighter or match and burn it. Yes, I said burn it. Truth is, whatever you wrote down on that paper was an excuse. It was some form of fear or doubt that has been keeping you and/or your partner from living the life that you want to live; the life that you've dreamed of. If you and/or your partner begin pursuing your dream(s) before you "think" you are "ready", what's the worst thing that can happen? Really think about it!

When it comes to dreams and goals you have to stop wishing for it, and start working towards it. Think about what you can do today. Even the smallest thing is a step in the right direction. Today is the only day guaranteed to you. That "someday" is never going to happen if you don't make it today. I believe that pursuing your dreams is what life is all about. Stop being irresponsible with your gifts and passions. Don't allow your partner to be irresponsible with their gifts and passions either. Don't wait until "someday".

You have to make a decision. Are your dreams and goals a priority? The answer should be yes. Yes my dreams are a priority;

and I owe it to my partner and myself to pursue them. It's critical that you realize that the time is now, be it days, hours, or even just minutes that you have to devote to your dreams. Ok, so there's not enough time in a day to do everything, but we all have the time to do something. Make the time you have work.

You and your partner have to choose to commit to your goals. Research, browse the internet, read a book on the subject, take a course, and even reach out to people who have achieved your goals. Obtaining a clear understanding of how others have achieved the same goal(s), will help each of you become better equipped to move forward. Don't allow your dreams and goals to become overwhelming. Break them down into smaller attainable tasks. Then celebrate each and every milestone you reach. Celebrating will boost your confidence and motivate you to stay focused. Having a partner can greatly help. You can inspire and push each other when one of you isn't feeling that good or lacks encouragement.

So what can you do today? You and your partner can take small steps as quickly as possible toward your goals. So you're wondering what does that mean. Look at what you and/or your partner know, whom you and/or your partner know, and any available resources. Maybe you have a friend that's a graphic designer, maybe you are a great writer, and maybe your partner is great at crunching numbers and budgeting. Utilize the resources you have directly around you to jump-start your road to success. Ask yourself what you can accomplish this week to make your goal closer to complete. Then get it done.

Having faith plays a big part in the process. Like I said before, there's no room to let doubt fester. Believe that you will achieve whatever you set out to do. You'll be amazed at how willing people are to help you along the way, if you believe in what you're trying to achieve. When people can see your passion they will gravitate to it and you. And make sure you show gratitude to those who provide support and guidance to your vision.

So here are the five key things to remember: (1) Stop waiting (2) Commit and pursue continuous action aligned to your goal(s) (3) Break your goal(s) out into smaller attainable milestones (4) Have faith and believe that you will get help along the way (5) Show sincere gratitude for any help received and any results attained.

## <u>Money or Time</u>

Everyday you wake up, go to a "job" that you dislike, put off your passion/goal until tomorrow, or make an excuse centered around not having enough time, remember the quick story above in this chapter. Everyday we put off our passion/goal we are either 1) helping someone else fulfill their passion/goal; 2) losing valuable time we have been blessed with by our Creator; or 3) misconstruing the value of time. What do I mean by misconstruing the value of time? Many people confuse "time for money" versus "money for time". The "clock puncher" or employee has been programmed to think that putting in time is the only way to make money (e.g., if my hourly wage is $10 per hour and I work 8 hours, I earned $80). They (i.e., the employee) become accustomed to working longer hours, leaving less time for other activities they may desire. The "clock checker" or successful employer plays by a different set of rules. The more they understand the power of time, the more they are willing to pay more money to obtain more time. They (i.e., the employer) understand the "processes and systems" philosophy of building businesses that can sustain with or without

OSCAR & KIYA FRAZIER

them being present. The successful employer doesn't spend "time" creating spreadsheets and reports. A small portion of their time and a large portion of their money is spent hiring the best and brightest talent. That talent is positioned in an environment that encourages leadership and rewards hard work. The employer then provides strategic vision, and empowers the newly hired talent to utilize their expertise to build lasting processes and systems. While the employees/talent are building best of breed processes and systems, the employer now has the time for business development, relationship building, and other ventures.

My partner and I had to apply this same "employer" concept to reaching our passion(s)/goal(s). When we first tried building nDemand Consulting, we tried being all things to all aspects of the organization (e.g., Human Resources, IT, Marketing, etc.). As the goal-owner, I found myself operating in the capacity of an instructor towards my partner, which led to several arguments and disagreements. Over time, we realized the value of investing in the best and brightest talent to build solid processes and systems. As they were built, we networked with other professionals, created lasting relationships, and found ourselves in more contract opportunities than ever before.

Whether you are setting up a business or simply trying to accomplish a goal, the same theories apply. Know your strengths, and proactively invest in hiring resources to bridge your weakness gaps. For example:

- You set a goal to lose weight, but you've never worked out before and nutrition is very confusing for you. Do you:

  a. Spend the next several months researching workout routines and nutrition plans; or

  b. Spend the next day or so researching fitness coaches that fit within your budget, and offer nutrition plans. Hire a fitness coach and spend the next several months seeing results.

## V. THE WEALTHIEST PLACE ON EARTH
### Die On "E"

At the end of every year my partner and I always set aside time to reflect over the year as it rolls to a close. We look at the things we set out to do, and the things that we didn't do and determine how those things align to our goals for the coming new year. By the end of 2012, it was clear to us that we hadn't been living. All those years prior to 2012 we merely existed. And now we are determined to live until we die. Before we started pursuing our dreams we allowed life to just happen to us, and now we've decided to take the wheel, let our passions and our faith be our guide. We decided to believe that we could achieve the things that we dreamed about, and even some things that we had not even thought about before. Our dreams began to wake us up in the morning, instead of keeping us up (awake) at night.

Understand I'm not telling you that this journey has been a walk in the park. Nor am I telling you that this journey is simple, and paved with gold and sugar flowers. We've had our arguments, ups and downs, and there are even times when we have to push and pull each other along the way. The great thing is we are living our dreams, and striving for many more. So, I say this to move you to act, because there is no reason why you and your partner should wait. The key is you have to be willing to step outside your comfort zone. You and your partner have to be willing to reach for what you never thought was possible. Believing in each other and taking action is half the battle.

Did you notice the title of this chapter? It was inspired by a quote my partner and I heard sometime ago while listening to one of our favorite motivational speakers, Les Brown. The quote goes something like this:

*"The graveyard is the richest place on earth, because it is here that you will find all the hopes and dreams that were never fulfilled, the books that were never written, the songs that were*

*never sung, the inventions that were never shared, the cures that were never discovered, all because someone was too afraid to take that first step, keep with the problem, or determined to carry out their dream."*

Powerful stuff huh! You can't take wealth with you to the grave (so they say), but you can take your unfulfilled dreams. Think about all the amazing things that could have been accomplished by so many people, had they just tried it, stuck with it, applied it, went for it, and believed that they deserved it. I've recently heard a few people say "die on empty". My partner and I are now officially applying this saying to how we live our lives. It is our hope that this motivates you, moves you, and inspires you and your partner to take action. I don't want to contribute any more wealth to the countless graveyards across this world.

## **Introspective Analysis**

When I was a kid, I watched my mother and father work hard; day after day – week after week – month after month – year over year. As I got older and out of the house, I would get calls every once in a while about an idea or concept they wanted to "invest in" or try; none of which came to fruition. It was difficult (and still is) to watch an 80-year-old man (in 2014) still talking about investing in something to bring to market and not taking proper strides to get it done. My dad's latest "concept" was to take his barbeque sauce to market and have it sold in stores. When he brought the idea to me, I immediately put on my small business development hat. "What will differentiate your sauce from competition?" "Do you know who your major competitors are?" "Do you have a plan for bottling and distribution?" And the list of questions went on. My dad grew frustrated with me as he didn't have answers to these questions, but felt he was ready to go to market.

Can you relate to having a lot of "ideas" or concepts that you've never acted upon? Have there been times when you looked over your life and realized there were so many things that you "should've", "would've", "could've" accomplished but something got in to the way of your progress? Well, you're not alone. This is a common occurrence with people, and [often times] an easy scapegoat when faced with the question "why didn't you just do it". Imagine with me for just a moment. Picture yourself as an Xbar on a normal-shaped bell curve (nerdy way of saying the middle ☺ )

and you are asked to equate three standard deviations to the left, and three standard deviations to the right of Xbar (another nerdy way of saying from the middle move three points back, and three points forward). Now, let's think of the Xbar as present time or your current point in life, and the three deviation points left and right as years moving in 5-year increments. Ask yourself the following questions:

1.  (Xbar) In my current life, am I where I want to be? Do I have the proper resources in my life to help me get to where I want to be?

2.  (first standard deviation to the left) Where was my life 5 years ago? Now, list at least three things you said you were going to do or accomplish, but did not. List the reasons why you didn't accomplish them.

3.  (second standard deviation to the left) Where was my life 10 years ago? Now, list at least two things you said you were going to do or accomplish, but did not. List the reasons why you didn't accomplish them.

4.  (third standard deviation to the left) Where was my life 15 years ago? Now, list at least one thing you said you were

going to do or accomplish, but did not. List the reason(s) why you didn't accomplish it.

5. Introspective Analysis: After reviewing the list of things you were going to do or accomplish, thoroughly read and digest the reasons why you didn't accomplish them over the last 5-10-15 years. Are some of the reasons similar or the same? Do you notice trends?

6. (first standard deviation to the right) Based on your current life, list at least three things you will accomplish in the next 5 years, using "I am" statements (e.g., in the next five years, I am a doctor; in the next five years, I am a parent with two children, etc. – we'll get to why the "I am" statement is so important in a later chapter). Now beside each of the three things you will accomplish, complete the following sentence: "I know five years ago, I had the following excuses: [refer back to step 2 above and fill in here]. Now, I am accepting responsibility for my life and those excuses are no longer a part of my life. I am whole, I am perfect, and I will succeed."

7. (second standard deviation to the right) Based on your life

in five years, list at least two things you will accomplish in the next 10 years, using "I am" statements. Now beside each of the two things you will accomplish, complete the following sentence: "I know ten years ago, I had the following excuses: [refer back to step 3 above and fill in here]. Now, I am accepting responsibility for my life and those excuses are no longer a part of my life. I've already accomplished the things I set out to do five years ago, and I will do the same thing now. I am whole, I am perfect, and I will succeed."

8. (third standard deviation to the right) Based on your life in ten years, list at least one thing you will accomplish in the next 15 years, using "I am" statements. Now beside the thing you will accomplish, complete the following sentence: "I know fifteen years ago, I had the following excuses: [refer back to step 4 above and fill in here]. Now, I am accepting responsibility for my life and those excuses are no longer a part of my life. I've already accomplished the things I set out to do ten years ago, and I will do the same thing now. I am whole, I am perfect, and I will

succeed."

Was the exercise above difficult or [seemingly unrealistic]? The final part of this exercise will be a bit uncomfortable because it requires you to picture yourself at death. All of the things you said you would do, but didn't – all of the things you planned to do, you can't – that great concept you had and kept pushing off for next year, is gone. How would you explain or list your excuses then? As earlier described, the wealthiest place on earth is the graveyard. Dreams unfulfilled; ideas dormant – forever. What will your legacy be; a person that left this world on "E" (i.e., empty), having fulfilled the things you want to do or accomplish? Or the person that left this world on "F" (i.e., full), having tons of unfulfilled things that went unaccomplished, with only a hope that it would have been great?

I choose to leave this world on "E". The Xbar and standard deviation exercise listed previously in this chapter I've done with my partner several times. It provides us an opportunity to look at our progress (or, in some cases, the lack there of) and diagnose symptoms that are holding us back. The statements created in this exercise should be placed somewhere that's easily accessible, in plain view, and referenced on an ongoing and consistent basis. Some may use a vision board; others may simply print the statements out and place them throughout their house or office. My partner and I put the statements on reminder alarms on our phones and have it set to alarm throughout the day; everyday. Eventually, the statements become engrained in our memory and results begin to take shape.

# VI. YOU'VE DECIDED TO TAKE THE LEAP, SO NOW WHAT?
## The Leap of Faith

It was the summer of 2009, my partner and I were living in Washington DC. We had hit a valley in our career which took a huge toll on our relationship as well. A lot of the people we considered "friends" proved themselves to be other than friends. The way we looked at life was starting to take a turn for the worse.

I called my sister (who was living in Charlotte, NC) to vent to her about all of the things going wrong in our lives. She listened, offered some advice, and allowed me to get all of my frustration out. She then asked me a simple question. "Do you read," she asked. I replied, "not as much as I used to." She then recommended a book called "The Secret" by Rhonda Byrne. I had not heard of the book, but my sister thought highly of the book and the message it delivered. I went to the bookstore later that day and picked it up. Within a couple of days, I completed the book and insisted that my partner read it.

"The Secret" teaches about the art of attraction – how thoughts become things – how we are what we think. My partner and I sat down several times to discuss the book's concept and how we were in desperate need of changing the way we think about our life and future. One day, I asked my partner about staying in Washington DC long-term (by this time, I'd been living in DC for just over four years and just shy of two years for my partner). My specific question was, "do you feel like DC can become home for you?" Surprisingly, DC was not a place my partner could ever call "home".

We sat in the living room for hours talking about the impacts of moving (e.g., costs, new jobs, career, etc.). At the time, I was making a nice six-figure salary and my partner wasn't far behind. By the end of the conversation, we narrowed our plan down to three cities (Charlotte, Dallas, and Houston). Weeks passed; vision boards created, modified, and modified again; then we decided on

Charlotte, NC because it presented the most positive energy for our lives.

A move like this was drastic for me. I was deeply rooted in government consulting and saw a clear path to expanding my market footprint. But it was not just about me. I had a partner that had a good career, but less-than-desired social life. I was finding myself getting caught up in the fast lane of money, partying, and materialism. Something had to give.

Fast-forward to February 2010, we were in a U-Haul truck with all of our belongings heading down to Charlotte, NC for a fresh start. Our adjustment was bumpy. I landed a job first and moved a month or so earlier than my partner. By mid-2010, we were both back in to the swing of corporate life. Yes, the pace was much slower than DC, but I welcomed it. My career quickly catapulted and I found myself in a good place.

Regardless of your "leap of faith", it is important to trust the art of attraction. As outlined in biblical terms (i.e., Proverbs), "as a man thinketh in his heart, so is he." In the previous chapter, we walked you through an exercise using "I am" statements. The power of the words "I am" exists in the affirmation you are releasing to the world when you follow up with the words after it. "I am successful" – "I am whole" – "I am unstoppable" – "I am healthy". And the list goes on. When you take the leap, speak life in to your destination. Eliminate all negative thoughts and only speak positive affirmations (i.e., "I am" statements). Couple this positivity with commitment to seeing it through, success will happen by default.

## The Challenge to Let Go

You and your partner have decided that you're tired of the excuses. The timing is never going to be right, so let's go for it. You're ready to stop doubting your abilities, stretch beyond your comfort zone, and start achieving your hearts desires and dreams. Regardless of how far along you are in the process, you understand that it's not going to be handed to you on a silver platter. If it were that easy, everyone would have done it already. However, take a moment to celebrate that you're here. Breathe it in, and buckle up. Never lose sight that there is a reason you are here. Regardless of the hurdles, obstacles, or walls, don't ever take your eye off the prize.

You've put in years to build a successful career; you've taken countless hours of training, only to realize that you're passionate about something totally different than your current job. It makes it very challenging to let go. What about everything you've built, or the name you've made for yourself? It's understandable that you're not ready to abandon the profession you've spent so much time pursuing. Was it all a waste? No! Trust me at some point those skills, and that logic you learned will come in handy. The only thing that would be a waste would be continuing down a path, with a profession that you're no longer passionate about. In the long run you're only denying what you really want.

There's going to come a moment when straddling the fence is no longer acceptable for you. The thing is, you have to be ready to consciously live your life on your terms. This means letting go and unlearning the things that have been imbedded in your brain about work vs. dreams. When you finally smash your fears, throw away those doubts, and dethrone the naysayers to be who you truly want to be, there will be no hurdle high enough to stop you.

## VII. 86,400 SECONDS

*"I have only just a minute, Only sixty seconds in it. Forced upon me, can't refuse it. Didn't seek it, didn't choose it. But it's up to me to use it. I must suffer if I lose it. Give account if I abuse it. Just a tiny little minute, but eternity is in it."* - Dr. Benjamin E. Mays

### Be Accounted For

I remember, as a child, having to wake up early in the morning, every morning, to sit and "think" with my dad. I never understood it, and I would always complain about it. My dad would say, "Laying in the bed all day is for dead people. The world will pass you by. Don't you know all important decisions are made before 8 o'clock in the morning?" We didn't always just sit there and think. My dad loved yard / garage sales and would get up at the crack of dawn to look for some that would pop up in or around our neighborhood. If there wasn't a yard or garage sale in the cold months, we'd get up early and chop wood out back. In the warm months, we'd do yard work. There was always work to be done when it came to early mornings with my dad.

But this instilled something in me. It taught me the value of getting up and being present. Now, as a successful entrepreneur, I pride myself in making just about all of my major decisions prior to 8 o'clock in the morning. After 8 o'clock in the morning, I'm implementing those decisions.

There are 86,400 seconds in a day – 1,440 minutes in a day – 24 hours in a day. How you chose to use that time is completely up to you. Did you know:

- between four and five people are born in the world every second?
- every three seconds, an area of the South American rain forest the size of a football field is cut down?
- Oprah Winfrey makes approximately $523 every minute?
- Everyday, your heart beats approximately 100,000 times?

The Bureau of Labor Statistics conducted a 2012-13 survey to determine the time used on an average work day for employed persons ages 25 to 54 with children. Here's the results:

- 7.7 hours: Sleeping
- 8.8 hours: Working & Related Activities
    - further data can be pulled to stratify the 8.8 hours of working & related activities to suggest that a large portion of the 8.8 hours are non-value added activity and non-work related.
- 2.6 hours: Leisure & Sports
- 1.6 hours: Other
- 1.2 hours: Caring for Others
- 1.1 hours: Eating & Drinking
- 1.0 hours: Household Activities

How does this data compare to your workday hour segmentation? Now, how often do you hear the words "I just don't have enough time"?

The fact of the matter is, you do have enough time! When it comes to fulfilling a passion/goal or taking a leap of faith in to something new, time can be your biggest asset or biggest hindrance. In the previous chapters, the output of some of the exercises provided should be "I am" statements, goal-oriented motivational lists, excuse-eaters, and more. Now, let's take a moment to discuss how we can help you find time to get it all done.

1. Step I: on a sheet of paper, write out how your work day is broken out (in hours) using the same categories provided previously in the Bureau of Labor Statistics data (e.g., sleeping; working & other related activities; leisure & sports; etc.).

2. Step II: beside each category, provide an answer to the following questions:

   a. this category a non-negotiable (i.e., must happen every work day)?

   b. If the category is a non-negotiable, can the hours be adjusted to free up more time?

   c. If the category is not a non-negotiable, can the category be moved to happen less frequently, freeing up more time during the work week?

d. If I change the hours or frequency of this category, what else will it impact?

3. Step III: Make adjustments to your categories and hours based on changes identified in step II.

## **<u>Productivity Schedule</u>**

So who invented the saying there's not enough time in a day? The trick is understanding how and where you're using your seconds, minutes, and hours. Now let me be the first to say, I'm not great at utilizing my time wisely every day. I'm still learning how to manage time effectively. I'm learning that planning ahead does wonders for how my days are conducted. Listing tasks, from the mundane to the critical, is a great way to get a handle on things to be accomplished each day. However, the key is effectively prioritizing the list.

Learn your productivity schedule. I'm more productive in the late afternoon and evening. While a lot of people are more productive in the morning. You have to learn yours and be honest with yourself. For example, don't start a very intricate task late in the day if your productivity peak is in the morning. You're only setting yourself up for procrastination.

I know too well how easy it is to get engulfed in a task and lose track of time. My partner and I have even experienced moments where we have so many deadlines that we will forget to take breaks. I've noticed that when we don't take breaks, and as we move from task to task, frustration and agitation will find its way into the room. Frustration and agitation reduces the quality of your work. Breaks are essential to your well being, and refreshing to your productivity.

## VIII. BEING RELENTLESS

*"Success isn't a finite resource; everyone can have it."* - The Law

of Attraction

### **Average Won't Get It**

This morning as I sat in bed and watched the sun come over the trees, my mind drifted to people I admire that have made a huge impact on this world. I thought about Oprah Winfrey, Nelson Mandela, Steve Jobs, and on and on. These are world-changing people from different walks of life. Then I started to think about these individuals and how each of them grew to greatness. Not one of them grew to greatness overnight. Each person spent years stretching beyond their comfort zone, learning and practicing his or her craft. Then, this thought came to me in that moment; *average isn't going to get it*. You have to do something above average, to achieve greatness. To reach your dreams you have to give it all you got, empty out everything holding you back, and go for it with every fiber of your being. You have to be relentless in your pursuit.

Relentless pursuit means, not giving up when the road gets hard or tiresome (this is going to happen, even if you're passionate). Relentless pursuit means facing issues and obstacles head on. Life is going to change; your world is going to change, because you're letting go of comfortable and normal to become extraordinary. Simply put, change is not easy. Relentless pursuit means, being patient and consistent. If you consistently do everything in your power to achieve your goal, your time will come. Relentless pursuit means going for your dreams, even when others don't get it, or think it's crazy. Surround yourself with people who are like-minded, people who are in relentless pursuit of their dreams as well. You'll find that like-minded go-getters are supportive, and resourceful. Anything short of a relentless pursuit of your goals will not cut it – it won't get you where you want to go.

We attract whatever we think about; good or bad. Whether or not you believe in the power of the universe, scientific research has proven that there are beneficial effects directly related with positive thinking. My partner and I have been practicing the law of attraction for several years; it works. We've been able to attract several wonderful, life-changing things to our lives, from simply believing that we deserved them, and thinking positively about them. At the very least, having a positive outlook on life gives you an extra boost to stay focused on seeing your goals/passions through.

## **At Your Core**

Throughout this book, you learned that the timing will never be perfect. You observed ways to include your partner in to pursuing your passion(s)/goal(s), as well as the dangers of not pursuing your passions at all. There have been real-life examples of things that have happened in my or my partner's life that helped us overcome fear. We provided a perspective on the value of time versus money. You learned the power of the "I am" statement, and how to find time to reach your destination.

Now, what about the inner you? There's no book that can truly speak to you, like you can speak to you! You've got to believe in yourself; your values – the core of who you really are. When no one else is around, and it's just you looking in the mirror, what keeps you going? What things are you able to look deep down inside at, and if you can find no other reason to keep going, this one thing can keep you strong? Take those things that motivate you and embrace them; hold them tight. There will be times when society and/or people will doubt your passion(s)/goal(s) or destinations. Trust the processes and systems you've built. Refer back to the "I am" statements you created. Release all of the excuses you had 5-10-15 years ago. Grab your life by the horns and take hold of every aspect of you.

When your time here on earth is gone, leave no dream/passion/goal left behind. Leave a legacy that your children's children will be proud of. Whether you're in a goal-owner or goal-supporter role in your relationship, remember communication is key. Let your partner know why they are needed in helping you reach your destination. And finally, don't be afraid of failure; but never settle for it. Grow stronger, get wiser, and learn how to get better.

There's a quote from Tecumtha, a Native American leader, that sends goose bumps (i.e., southern dialect for chills ☺) through me every time I read it. It speaks of respect, honor, and no fear of leaving this natural life. As a close to this book, I'd like to leave you with Tecumtha's words in hopes that it encourages you to be the best.

*"So live your life that the fear of death can never enter your heart. Trouble no one about their religion; respect others in their view, and demand that they respect yours. Love your life, perfect your life, beautify all things in your life. Seek to make your life long and its purpose in the service of your people. Prepare a noble death song for the day when you go over the great divide. Always give a word or a sign of salute when meeting or passing a friend, even a stranger, when in a lonely place. Show respect to all people and grovel to none. When you arise in the morning give thanks for the food and for the joy of living. If you see no reason for giving thanks, the fault lies only in yourself. Abuse no one and no thing, for abuse turns the wise ones to fools and robs the spirit of its vision. When it comes your time to die, be not like those whose hearts are filled with the fear of death, so that when their time comes they weep and pray for a little more time to live their lives*

*over again in a different way. Sing your death song and die like a*

*hero going home."*

# ABOUT THE AUTHORS

Oscar Lamont Frazier is the owner of nDemand Consulting LLC, a strategy, marketing, and execution firm headquartered in Charlotte NC. He graduated from Johnson C. Smith University with a B.S. degree in Business Administration, concentration in Management. Years later, he graduated from Strayer University with a M.B.A degree, concentration in Management. Mr. Frazier has provided executive coaching and motivational team coaching for several small businesses and prides himself in making an impact in the entrepreneurial space. Mr. Frazier is a member of Omega Psi Phi Fraternity Inc. (Rho Chapter), and the Free & Accepted Masons (F&AM) Fraternity (Heart to Heart Lodge No. 597).

Kiya Dowdy Frazier is a Sr. Marketing Consultant and Co-owner of nDemand Consulting LLC, with over a decade of relevant experience specializing in strategic communications, logistics planning, and brand management. A graduate of Johnson C. Smith University, Kiya has a B.A. in Mass Communications, with a concentration in Public Relations and Marketing. She later went on to obtain her M.B.A in Marketing from Strayer University. Throughout her career she has been responsible for managing the editing, updating, and designing of marketing materials including contract proposals, brochures, and a wide variety of client deliverables for multiple clients. She has boosted productivity and fostered efficiencies in various settings. Kiya is a wife, entrepreneur, philanthropist, musician, and proud owner of a Boxer named Apollo. She lives in Charlotte, NC.

www.ingramcontent.com/pod-product-compliance
Lightning Source LLC
LaVergne TN
LVHW021544080426
835509LV00019B/2822